Sun Country

Elegant

Sun Country Elegant

Patricia Hart McMillan

GIBBS·SMITH
P
PUBLISHER

SALT LAKE CITY

First Edition

04 03 02 01 00   5 4 3 2 1

Published by
Gibbs Smith, Publisher
P. O. Box 667
Layton, UT 84041

Orders: (1-800) 748-5439
Visit our Web site at *www.gibbs-smith.com*

Edited by Gail Yngve
Designed by CN Design
Printed and bound in Hong Kong

Library of Congress Cataloging-in-Publication Data

McMillan, Patricia Hart.
Sun country elegant / Patricia Hart McMillan.—1st ed.
p. cm.
ISBN 1-58685-002-4
1. Interior decoration—United States. 2. Decoration and ornament, Rustic—United States. I. Title.

NK2002 .M419 2000
747—dc21   00-029147

iv

Jacket Front: Vibrant blue walls and painted white floors are a delightful background for an eclectic mix of furnishings in artist Alexandra Lotsch's country-house living room.

Jacket Back: Alexandra Lotsch's whimsical painted picnic table sets a casually elegant tone for the den of her remodeled Long Island country house.

Half-Title Page: Simpson's Advent door opens to a stunning window treatment inside and a simply elegant porch outside.

Title Page: French-country-style furniture by Milling Road—undraped French windows and an abundance of blooms—speak volumes about the new country-house style that's no longer about farms and farmhouses.

Opposite: Richard and Stephanie Sterns' sixteenth-century English-barn dining room in the Berkshires goes elegantly with Louis XVI–style chairs and an antique faïence pattern by Lunéville, France's oldest existing pottery.

Epigraph Page: Designer Susan Zises Green's lavish window treatment adds elegance to a country study.

Dedication Page: Richard and Stephanie Sterns' country-house living room was once an English barn.

Contents Page: A sumptuous plaid sofa and comfy chair in a lively cabbage-rose pattern from the Lillian August Collection for Drexel-Heritage re-create an English manor-house mood. The wrought-iron garden table adds a just-right relaxed touch.

And *because I cannot promise*
any more myself,
(save the long fatigue, great diligence,
and the love that I have bestowed
to understand and practice what I now offer,)
if it pleases God that I may not have laboured in vain,
I shall heartily thank his goodness;
acknowledging withal, myself obliged to those,
that from their beautiful inventions,
and from the experience they had,
have left the precepts of such an art,
because they have opened a more easy and
expeditious way to the discovery of new things,
which perhaps had otherwise been hid.

—Andrea Palladio

*Dedicated to*

Richard and Stephanie Stern,

who built something elegant

Contents

Swedish furniture designer Martine Colliander looks to antiqued white furniture, such as her own Solgarden Collection for Lexington, and light interiors to brighten winter-weary rooms. Accessories are kept light and cheerful.

Changing Country

In decorating, as in life, nothing stays the same. Happily, change is not only inevitable but often most rewarding. I recall the point at which I realized that I was witnessing a profound change from Early American to what could truly be called "American Country." To me, it signified a strong rejection of both the over-decorated, pretentious-home life-style and the sterility of the glass, steel, and chrome hi-tech.

My love of country began while building a simple sugarhouse barn in Vermont, getting to know the rural landscape and village people. For me, it was a natural step to create the concept for a new magazine, *Country Living*. The first issue was on the newsstand in July 1978. I was thrilled at the response and so was the publisher, Hearst. I was tapped to move to *House Beautiful* as its editor-in-chief, and I handed the new magazine into the hands of caring others.

The appeal of American Country style soon became apparent. In early 1980, within weeks of one another, two books on the new style appeared. First came *Decorating Country Style*, by Patricia Hart McMillan and Rose Bennett Gilbert, editors at *1,001 Decorating Ideas* magazine. Within a few days, *American Country Style*, authored by Mary Emmerling, appeared in bookstores.

At *House Beautiful*, we began to devote many issues to traditional country styles from around the world. I found my clear favorite to be Swedish Country. That fascination with Scandinavian design resulted in the publishing of my book in 1991, *Scandinavian Country*.

Today, we continue with the exciting evolution of country style and embrace its many facets. With country decorating tastes moving toward the use of classical elements, *Sun Country Elegant* proves once again that there is something new under the always-changing decorating sun.

—JoAnn R. Barwick
Former editor-in-chief, *House Beautiful*
Founding editor, *Country Living*

Oleg Cassini's grand country house, originally the home of Louis Comfort Tiffany, is on Long Island's North Shore.

Grand Country

Mine has always been the world of elegant country homes—in France, where I was born and lived in my youth; in Italy, where I studied as a young man; in California, where I became a costume designer to filmdom's most beautiful stars; and on Long Island's lovely North Shore, a place of grand country homes of real people as well as F. Scott Fitzgerald's imaginary immortal Daisy and Gatsby. Beautiful in its pure classical elegance, my house—built by the legendary Louis Comfort Tiffany—is not the glitzy status house of Fitzgerald's imagination. In the best tradition of the ancient villa, my country house is a spiritual retreat, the place to which I hurry from cares of the city. It's a place where nature surrounds and soothes, where my faithful dogs and delightful miniature horses find refuge.

Because my house itself is pleasingly designed, its classical lines destined to be always in style and enduringly elegant, one might think of it as quintessentially "elegant sun country." It is elegant. It warms to the sun in every season. In a certain sense, it is a world apart—a bit of heaven, exactly what the traditional grand country house or villa was intended to be—paradise reclaimed.

Today, creating one's grand country place has to do with an attitude of respect for and pride in place. It has to do with imbuing a dwelling, no matter how small, with an elevating sense of dignity, the most basic element of elegance, at home with every architectural style. It is easy to understand one's desire to seek a country house, open it to the sun, and add civilizing refinement. Little wonder that we are witnessing the emerging elegant sun-country style. In extolling well-appointed interiors that open graciously to the glories of nature, this new decorating style carries on the noblest traditions of the historic grand country house.

—Oleg Cassini

The Elegant House

THE MYTH AND THE MAGIC The days of formality may be gone forever. Certainly, ceremony and ritual may have disappeared into a vast chasm of casualness, but despite the penchant for comfort—part and parcel of the American character, some philosophers say—there is a decided return to elegance. Fashion designers are trimming denim in beads. And the relaxed American Country decorating style, a favorite since its recognition in the late '70s, is giving way to more sophisticated, sun-loving contemporary interiors. Call it casual elegance. Call it elegant sun country style. Why the

---

*Elegant: tastefully fine or luxurious
in dress, style, design; gracefully refined and dignified;
pleasingly superior in quality.*

millennial move from farmhouse to manor house? There are probably many answers to this question. Prosperity must be among the most important reasons. But, despite the natural inclination to improve one's living conditions along with one's income, prosperity is not the only answer.

Elegance is not merely a matter of money. It is an attitude. Discernment and taste make it possible to create something wonderful from simple materials. The late Sister Parish demonstrated this so beautifully when she painted an unmatched collection of chairs white and placed them in a room of cheerful, colorful country fabrics in her summer home. What a powerful visual lesson.

Taste is something always growing, always changing as we see and learn more. Perhaps that is one reason elegance is returning. We've seen more and learned something new. And now, to demonstrate that we've learned elegance, we create something elegant. It seems a perfectly natural sequence.

But none of these reasons is the whole answer. The eagerness for elegance more likely has its roots in myth, or that which causes us to seek and recognize the familiar in our effort to return to Eden. We remember the grand villas created by such ancients as Palladio, patron saint of architects. The great country houses were designed to suit their sites but at the same time to command them. The structures were meant to be places of enormous pleasure—for re-creation of the spirit—as the inhabitants communed with restorative nature in a kind of paradise. These houses show economy of design and are renowned for their classic excellence. Palladio studied each site, noting the direction of the winds, the movement of light across the land, and ease of access by water and by land. Windows were planned with concern for the composition of fenestration and facade so that light moved into and around rooms. No detail was unimportant. "God is in the details," Mies van der Rohe, an architect following Palladio, said. Beauty and elegance, kinds of truth, are in the details. Details are a result

Previous Page: The furniture looks French, but painted board floors and simple painted moldings create a mood that is uniquely sun country and especially American in artist Alexandra Lotsch's Long Island country house.

Above: Lunéville's ZaZa faïence tea set is at home with a Louis XVI chair, casually covered in white duck.

of thought, not money. Money may make a "great pile," as they call big stone houses in England, but thoughtfulness makes a beautiful, dignified house. Here, in *Sun Country Elegant*, we offer food for thought with diverse homes that are the result of work by talented homeowners, interior designers, and some of America's leading architects. Collectively, their work demonstrates that excellence and elegance go hand in hand. 🎵

Part One

GREAT PLACES IN THE SUN

CUSTOMIZING COUNTRY   *Elegant homes in diverse forms and different places reach out to sun, sky, and water.* Once, the city dictated fashion. Country copied city style without proper tools, using only local materials. The result, provincial style, was considered crude, unsophisticated, and undesirable. Today, the same design genius often works simultaneously in town and country since turnabout is fair play, bringing country design ideas to the city. Choices of materials and tools are no longer limited to immediate areas but may come from anywhere in the world. The result is exciting country houses that are sophisticated and elegant. Elegance, an aesthetic that is mostly a matter of doing the right thing, does not depend on expensive materials or large size. Several of the larger homes here, derelicts when their owners discovered them, were lovingly remodeled. Now, they're dignified and imposing—elegant—but, at the same time, replete with country comforts. Several homes, planned and built with economy in mind, could rightly be called shacks. Their owners, perhaps with tongue-in-cheek, often refer to them in that way. Nonetheless, these homes express decidedly elegant simplicity, efficiency, and ease. All of these houses, even the courtyard house in a city, reach out to nature, inviting all who visit to feel equally at home and at ease in the truly elegant sun-country style.

20

A bronze statue lends a touch of formality to the gardens at Reynolda.

Southern Comfort

A decorative courtyard creates a sense of country in the city. The garden retains its unmanicured country look, but the house has undergone changes to become as comfortably elegant "as a pair of old but still-favorite shoes," says Pilar. "The L-shaped house was very simple, so my husband [artist Julio Larraz] and I added a wing, creating a courtyard. We enclosed the courtyard area with a wall that has unglazed windows covered with wooden balusters. We added a loggia that wraps around the house inside the courtyard, creating protection from the sun and rain. Now, doors opening onto the

It was not the house; it was the two-and-one-half acres of land wildly covered in avocado, mango, orange, and grapefruit trees that was so beautiful. And, only minutes from downtown Miami.

—Pilar Larraz, industrial designer

loggia can remain open to breezes and traffic. The courtyard also provides a protected area in which our children can play." Adding the enclosed courtyard transformed the house into a typical Spanish Colonial country style, a style rooted in Roman design. Pilar says, "The courtyard allows us to be inside but feel as though we are outside. It gives good balance between inside and outside." On the back side of the house, a new deck outside the dining room leads to a backyard pool. French doors open from the master bedroom onto this deck.

Pilar and Julio mixed, indeed created, the paint that covers the exterior of the house. The base is whitewash, like that used for country houses in Pilar's native Colombia. The unique golden yellow color comes from mineral-powder pigments usually added to cement. "We found it in a hardware store," she says. The idea of adding a blue stripe to the exterior courtyard wall also came from similar treatments Pilar had seen in Colombia. The green door is perhaps unexpected, but it, too, is a deliberate country touch. "Country folk have fewer color prejudices. They're more free in their use of color," she says.

Pilar and Julio named their house *La Casurina*, Spanish for the Australian pine trees that grow abundantly on their land, and furnished it with country pieces from flea markets and antiques stores. Pilar's favorites—simple, heavy, Spanish-style tables—mix with other styles and periods with aplomb. The overall effect is stylish, "but the simpler, the better," says Pilar. "We put things wherever we like and constantly rearrange so that the house is in permanent renewal."

Page 22: Wicker chairs add Victorian elegance to a shaded courtyard.

Previous Pages: A Chippendale sofa and eighteenth-century drop-leaf table bring traditional colonial-style elegance to the Larraz living room.

Below: This handsome door opens onto the easy elegance of a tiled courtyard.

Opposite: A Windsor rocker adds unexpected country charm to a cozy corner of the loggia, decorated as though it were a casually dressy entry hall.

Above: A New England–like Windsor settle and rush-bottomed ladder-back chairs coexist happily with antique farm implements from South America in a corner of the Larrazes' shuttered courtyard. Plank shutters close out inclement weather.

High Plains Drifting

"Stone has an immediacy to it because of the animation of its visual surface, and, at the same time, it is timeless," says architect Bartholomew Voorsanger, who designed a mostly stone house in Wyoming. The site flanks the Wind River Range of the Continental Divide. His clients, conservationists, planned the 12,000-square-foot house as a retreat for intimate family events and holidays. "Following the tradition of the villa—a house with a grand vista—one drives miles past meadows, seeded each year with wildflowers, to get to the top of this retreat. It's a place where the owners can totally participate

Natural materials used with elegant simplicity focus the attention on nature in Big Sky Country.

Glints of sparkling sunlight bounce off the lively stone chosen by architect Bartholomew Voorsanger for both the interior and exterior of this High Plains of Wyoming home, relieving the sense of austerity but none of its elegant linearity. Clerestory windows and glass walls admit light and endless views of land and sky from every room—especially the kitchen, opposite.

in the landscape. This really is Big Sky Country—they can see hail, snow, thunderclouds, and sunshine, all within a couple of hours," he says.

Stone for the house, Connecticut gneiss, anchors the structure to its high-plains site. Glass walls—the one in the living room is thirty feet long—liberate it, opening the house to vistas of unending sky, mountains, and flower-filled meadows. Electronically controlled blinds, usually used only when the family departs, lower at the flick of a switch.

Below: Great walls of glass open all rooms, including the bedrooms, to sweeping panoramas of meadows and mountains.

Opposite: Natural stone, soothing colors, and Shaker-simple lines combine to create a contemporary country house that uniquely embraces both modern and historic design references. Decoration plays second fiddle to the view.

Color is not schemed in the sense that it is applied or layered on. It emanates from natural materials without and within. The golden stone contains warm grays and a rich garnet, enlivened by flecks of glittering mica. "It is an active stone," observes Voorsanger. Wood contributes both color and contrasting texture. Voorsanger chose a butternut color for the ceilings, olive wood for the floors, and claro, a California crotch walnut, for the walls.

Contemporary furnishings, like the structure itself, are clean lined and unfussy, granting nature center stage.

Tropical Retreat

Even new houses in Key West have a certain tropical country ease and elegance. ❧ It has to do with tall, two-story-high ceilings, breeze-admitting French doors, windows that open onto charming verandas and terraces, and cool hushed interiors. "This house was built where a naval base once stood," says Juan Carlos Menendez, interior designer and architect with Taylor & Taylor, who designed the house. "It takes its cues from a nearby house owned by Calvin Klein, but, generally, the style emanated from the North and was adapted for the tropics." Menendez says that there is a certain quaintness to the way the

Pale interiors and plantation-style furnishings give this house in the tropics colonial cool.

Previous Page: French doors in the two-story-high living room of this Florida Keys house by Taylor & Taylor open onto a terrace.

Above: Bare is beautiful—and very country—in this dining room with its polished wood-plank floor and curtainless windows.

house sits on the site. The facade is not completely flat, but there is a bay and a terrace that wrap around the back. Inside, the living room occupies a two-story-high space. On the second floor, bedrooms flank the space, and each has a window that overlooks the living room. The master-bedroom suite is at the front of the second floor.

Taylor & Taylor found places for the owners' interesting collections. "There are fascinating fans," says Menendez. "There are ceiling fans and floor fans. We called one in the kitchen the chopper-slicer-dicer because the paddles changed from a down to an out position, depending on

whether the fan was on or off." Antique telephones, another passion of the collectors, were put to use throughout the house.

Phyllis Taylor keyed furnishings to the casual theme of the house. The sisal rug in the family room is hand painted with a braided-rope motif. In the dining room, backs of host and hostess chairs are upholstered in Madagascar, a pliable woven grass (or grass cloth) that is used as wall covering in the master bedroom and bath. This approach—upholstering formal furniture in an informal, casually chic fabric—is quintessential elegant sun-country style. 🌿

Previous Page: Wooden louvered shutters and Venetian blinds redirect too-bright sunlight in a cozy niche, where a long wooden table doubles as a desk. A high-tech lamp adds a contemporary touch. Pillows play up country comfort.

Opposite: A sheltered veranda fitted with teak deck chairs invites lazy lounging and long, leisurely views of surrounding gardens.

Above: A white picket fence and shallow front yard carry on the Key West architectural tradition, belying the contemporary country-house charm behind the entry door with its handsome oval-shaped glass panel.

Mountain Greenery

"When we discovered it, the Adirondack mountain house was a wonderful wreck, like a ruined castle," says Susan Zises Green. "We could tell by the date carved into the stone chimney that the long rectangular house, flanked by two square masses, had been built in 1922. The bluestone house was enormous, with eleven fireplaces and a twenty-six-foot-wide living room. The dining room was large enough for two seven-foot sofas, a chaise, and a table that seated thirty! "The house was also eccentric. There were his and hers dressing rooms with his initials carved into the wood. A bath with a copper tub connected the two

In the country castle that
Susan Zises Green saved, she elegantly mixes rich
gypsy-like color and pattern.

Previous Page: Designer Susan Zises Green created a living room that is at once elegant and exuberant.

Above: Removing a dropped ceiling revealed exciting original artwork in the Greens' kitchen.

dressing rooms. A pantry in the kitchen was covered in beautiful tiles. When we remodeled the kitchen, that area became our laundry. When pulling out the plaster kitchen ceiling to install insulation, we discovered incredible paintings on an earlier peaked ceiling. We surmised that the

Susan Zises Green's Recipe for Mixing and Matching Marvelously

Susan Zises Green, ASID, says that she loves all colors and has no favorites. She finds cream restful, dark green very restful, and green-blue—the color of the ocean—most restful. "I'm very flexible," she says. "I like lots of different things going on in a room." She seems to mix furniture and fabrics with a rich and elegant abandon. But, there's method to that seeming madness. Here are seven of Susan's super secrets.

1. Use furniture that has meaning. Even if your great-grandmother's chair is ugly, with a new cover it will look fabulous in your room. I have one chair that I've recovered three different times.

2. Don't throw it out, use it! Move everything in.

3. Mix different scales.

4. Mix motifs—paisley, stripes, floral prints.

5. Pick whimsical patterns that make you smile or feel warm and cozy.

6. Mix unusual colors, such as lavender and cream with coral.

7. Please your eye! Don't ask your friends. You are the one living in your house!

The bedrooms above and opposite show how a master of "the mix," Susan Zises Green, adds patterns aplenty, terrific textures, and a multitude of styles and periods in her inimitable style of classy country.

original owner had been a painter, that this room had been his studio and the pantry his kitchen. Unwilling to cover up these marvelous paintings, we put on a new roof.

"Over time, the chestnut planks on the living room walls had turned a hideous color. I actually had a dream about how to clean them. First, I numbered each of the 103 planks, removed them from the wall, and laid them on the lawn. I bought A&B solution at the local hardware store.

Using a paint roller, I covered the planks in the solution. Following the directions carefully, I bleached the planks, which were then reinstalled.

"Furnishing the house meant attending auctions and shopping at tag sales and flea markets here, there, and everywhere. I mix different patterns and styles. All people travel, bring things back, and mix them. It's a little like cooking—a little of this and a little of that! Today's houses reflect that philosophy.

"Once the very heart of a working farm, this great house became our escape from the city. It proved wonderful for entertaining a lot or a few people," says Susan.

Barn Beautiful

For the first twenty years of its busy life, Richard and Stephanie Stern's south-Berkshires weekend getaway—two-and-one-half hours and a world away from their hectic New York City life—was a cozy cottage. Over the years, it became clear that the house needed expansion to accommodate family and a growing circle of friends. The Sterns wanted no ordinary addition. "We learned about a sixteenth-century English barn imported by a regional builder. We purchased the unique timber framing, said to have been salvaged from decommissioned ships. Then we looked for just the right architect to integrate

A sixteenth-century English barn is transported and transformed.

the small one-story cottage and the large two-story-high barn. John James, a former New York City professor, accepted the challenge," Richard says.

"Getting the two structures to look as though they belonged together was the biggest problem," says James. His elegant solution—moving the driveway to the rear, excavating to create a three-car garage below the new structure, and siting the barn's low wall toward the street—is disarming. Visitors step through the front door of what looks like a handsome rambling country house and discover that they're in a barn—a 24-foot-wide-by-40-foot-long room with a soaring 24-foot-high ceiling. They gasp in surprise and delight, first at the enormous space, then at the captivating pattern of the timbers, and, finally, through a beautiful window wall to the mountains beyond. At one end of the room, there is a handsome brick fireplace with a raised hearth. At the opposite end of the room, the Gothic barn with classic fenestration opens to a long modern kitchen that occupies what was formerly a two-car garage and an enclosed back porch that served as a dining room. The space above the old garage yielded a bonus—an open loft area overlooking the barn and a very private guest room with its own bath. The stair and loft, protected by contemporary iron railings, form a transition between barn and cottage, making it reminiscent of a silo.

Working as a decorating team, Richard and Stephanie Stern and designer Pat McMillan created a thoroughly comfortable, dignified but not stuffy interior. In the barn, pale yellow walls with a mere hint of spring green—the kind one notices in budding willows—form a clean but not severe contrast with the weathered timbers. No art hangs on the timbers—they are art enough! Window and other trims are painted a pale gray that softly relates the yellow wall and aged timbers. The same subtle gray covers the walls of the adjoining kitchen. "There was no need to cover

Previous page: Designer Patricia Hart McMillan fearlessly mixes fancy furniture from several centuries in the Sterns' sixteenth-century barn addition. Underfoot and equally elegant is Wilsonart's wood-look laminate plank flooring.

Above: Modern ease prevails in the kitchen, where Gibraltar countertops by Wilsonart, Shaker-style cabinets from American Woodmark, and tempered-glass chairs by Curvet pull up to the peninsula with its inset gameboard.

Previous page: Raymond Waites designed the luxe-for-lounging upholstery in this living room. The over-scaled coffee table is an oxcart from Asian Antiques in Great Barrington. Ceramic teapots lining the mantel were handcrafted by the New Mexico artist Marianna Roumell-Gasteyer. All come together in a very personal sun-country style.

Below: Architect John James artfully blended a sixteenth-century English barn and an existing Berkshires cottage. First-time visitors are delighted to discover the beautiful barn that is the new living room with a window wall open to the sun.

the windows, so we left them bare—the better to enjoy the light and the mountain vistas that we love," says Stephanie.

The dark oak-look flooring is practical Wilsonart laminate. It stands up to the constant in-and-out traffic to the swimming pool in summer and cross-country skiing in winter. The floor is pet-friendly—important because the Sterns' dogs, Sam and Doug, have free run of the barn.

Weekend guests—exhausted from the pace of the city—sink blissfully into a cushy oversized sofa and chairs designed by Raymond Waites. Grouped around the fireplace and upholstered in soft greens and apricots, the seating area is an island in an ocean of calm. No tall furniture disturbs the serene balance established by the intriguing design of the timbers.

At the opposite end of the room, guests seem to fit comfortably at the round, marble-topped, teak dining table discovered in Great Barrington's Asian Antiques shop, where it languished because of its huge size. The ten fancy-glazed Louis XV chairs—scorned by auction-goers looking for New England antiques—were bought for a song. Chair seats were re-covered in vaguely ethnic-looking fabric in a woven geometric pattern.

A "waste not, want not" principle prevailed throughout barn and cottage. Familiar furnishings, valued for sentiment's sake, were freshened with new covers and finishes. Family and friends who gathered there in May 1999 to celebrate the marriage of the Sterns' daughter, Alison, to Aaron Simard delighted in the new but relished recognizing favorite old pieces and reminiscing about good times past. With this enduringly beautiful barn, the great promise is that the best is yet to be.

☙

Forest Glen

Typical New England country houses and churches are sided in white clapboard. But this is not the case with Vance Hosford's award-winning country home, which blends the ideas of both residence and church. It comes replete with a chapel, that, together with a porch, projects transept-like off an octagon at one end of the building. "I wanted a very bright interior, so I turned the color scheme inside out. I made the exterior dark brown and the interior light," Hosford says. Throughout, interior walls feature different tints of white with deep tones of dark blue-gray and Tuscan terra-cotta or light tints of soft

An award-winning house is colored to blend with the surrounding woods.

Previous page and above: Letting in light so that it adds to the sense of mystery and magic in his woodland home was beautifully planned and executed by architect Vance Hosford. Windows remain understated and bare.

gray-greens with pale ochres accentuating niches. Hosford uses white sparingly "because it is energetic," he says. Wood trim throughout is lightly textured oak or pine.

Above: In architect Hosford's hands, windows do not have to be big to be beautiful, nor do they need ostentatious treatments to seem elegant. Having no window treatment on this rectangular window allows the sunlight to stream in, lighting a corner bookshelf.

Enamored with light and the sense of wonder and animation that it brings, Hosford designed his cathedral-like home—in which some rooms have 30-foot-high ceilings—to be a receptacle of light. In the great

Above: Dark siding distinguishes this country house from traditional white farmhouses and allows the structure to blend into surrounding greenery.

Opposite: An ingenious wall-hung sundial adds a touch of whimsy and convenience for the gardener.

room, for example, he installed twenty casement windows to allow light to flood the room. In other rooms, he used the same kind of window in varying configurations.

For interior lighting, Hosford looked to sculpture-like sconces fitted with dimmers that allow lighting to be switched from a romantic nighttime mood, to a daytime indoor mood, to that of the bright outdoors. While the inside of this intriguing house seems sunny, the exterior disappears into the trees—but not from the view of *Metropolitan Home* editors, who named it a winner in the magazine's 1999 Met Home of the Year Contest.

Safe Harbor

Robert and Carol Swift's idyllic, white-clapboard house

by the harbor was far from picture pretty when they first saw it.

A run-down wreck, it had been a three-family home with

porches that had been enclosed as sunrooms. Now, because of

the Swifts' efforts, its easygoing elegance is obvious, and its

newly opened porches invite lazy-day gatherings. Unlike

their former house, this one has big rooms and high ceilings.

"There's a lot more light. We wanted to bring in that glorious

old summerhouse feeling. Friends asked what we would do with

our old things. Use them, of course! They work perfectly," says

The Swifts rescued
a harbor-side house, giving both home
and rescuers safe haven.

Previous page and above: Simplicity adds dignity so that cottage charm gains élan in the Swifts' living room and dining room. Bright colors and loads of sunlight spilling through curtainless windows spell sun country.

Bright colors, graphic patterns, and absence of clutter point to the new direction of today's dressed-up country decorating, where comfort is most important.

Carol, whose decorating philosophy is "Combine everything in your soul when you are doing a house." So she brought antiques, folk art, and quilts from their former home and a shop she owned. But, she says, if there's one thing she knows, it's when to stop! "I like a sparse look," she admits.

Carol Swift mixes antiques and other furnishings with aplomb. Her secret for success is the careful editing of her collection for a clean contemporary feeling.

Walls in the living and dining rooms are painted pale apricot. "We brought color from ceiling to floor by painting floor moldings the same apricot as the walls," says Carol. All other trim is a crisp country white. The pastel walls create an appealing backdrop for the Swifts' collections.

"This house and garden are so easy," says Carol. "The roses love the salt air and do amazingly well, blooming into early fall." Carol, who loves working in her garden, says, "I'm looking at the sea, working with the roses, and the raspberries are growing." What could be better? ❧

Above: A classic clapboard, this house by the harbor is now idyllic, thanks to the tender loving care of Robert and Carol Swift.

Opposite: Carol sets the table for a leisurely lunch al fresco on the porch with a splendid view of boats bobbing on the sparkling blue waters of the bay. A medley of furniture styles places emphasis on ease.

Marsh Magic

An environmentally protected salt marsh is a mood-making

setting for a playfully elegant country house built by William and

Pamela Richards. Architect Stanley F. Nielsen based the design

loosely on a Chesapeake lighthouse, replete with a copper-clad

windowed cupola. Because of building requirements, the tiny

clapboard house conforms to the footprint of an earlier clam

shack that stood on the site. The open-plan first floor combines

living, dining, and kitchen spaces with a wall of windows and

glass doors that provide continuous views of marsh life. A deck

overhanging the marsh runs the length of the tiny clapboard house and

Elegant whimsy enriches and enlivens a moody marsh.

wraps around one side, creating a ramp to the road. A spiral staircase that soars past a two-story bay window—the only window facing the road—takes visitors to the second floor. On this floor, tucked under eaves, are two children's bedrooms. Two steps up is the master bedroom with its own deck

overlooking the marsh. White walls and ceilings and exposed natural-wood beams and posts throughout emphasize elegant, modern architectural lines inside and nature's constantly changing show of color outside. Pickling gives the pine-plank flooring a warm and weathered look. Unexpectedly dressy and traditional furnishings are a delightful reference to the area's rich history. 🔊

Page 72: A New England marsh provides a unique country setting for a small weekend getaway.

Opposite: A wall of glass opens the master bedroom to spectacular views. Inside, decoration is simple and soothing.

Above: Traditional furniture is a charming counterpoint to its contemporary setting.

Seaside Serenity

This seaside dwelling is a perfect example of elegant simplicity and country-life privacy. Outside, the austere 18-by-28-foot rectangle is clad in gray shingles and enhanced by a simple deck. Inside, walls are reclaimed wood boards, "bleached, so as not to look Adirondack style," says architect Michael Prodanov. "No plasterboard," the vigorous, eighty-year-old client who commissioned the building had said. "But, for contrast, I backed the library wall and stairwell with drywall—gypsum board—painted white. Flooring is pine planking with exposed nail heads that create a pattern. The effect of this

Solitary splendor sets off a gem by the shore.

interior is clean, sparse, and elegant—the way you feel after you come out of a nice shower," says Prodanov.

Above: Colorful books and cushion covers accentuate the light neutral scheme without disturbing the calm throughout this seaside retreat.

The ground floor is one big room, which includes the kitchen and a private bath. There is no dishwasher and only a small refrigerator. The second floor is one immense bedroom. The deck off the bedroom is fitted with two levels of sunscreen and a stair that leads to the rooftop for evening stargazing.

Page 76: A pergola above the deck adds romance entirely in keeping with the simple design of this dwelling by the sea.

Above: Inside the one-room space, slipcovered chairs group convivially around the generous coffee table.

Tree House

"It's not a villa, but it feels like one. It's a sculpture—and such a pleasure to be in," says Susan Jennings, a student of architecture, about the jewel-box structure that she and architect Peter McMahon designed and built themselves over several summers. The house nestles into a wetland forest. "We cut as few trees as possible. One even comes through the deck," says Peter, who describes the house as loose, informal, experimental, unusual, outrageous, and "like an upside-down boat." The arched roof shields and protects the house, which is open to forest views through a wall of salvaged windows. Many

An elegant window wall creates an open-air feeling in a tree house.

Previous page: Found building materials and a decorating scheme borrowed from the sixties all look refreshingly new in the hands of collaborators McMahon and Jennings.

Above: Efficiency and economy, streamlining principles, mandated wall-hung shelves, and a built-in banquette leave floor space open.

materials and furnishings—exterior cedar siding, tongue-and-groove pine ceiling planks that will gray with age, laminated ceiling beams, appliances, glass bathroom shelving—were discerningly salvaged, scavenged, and recycled. Other items, such as the exterior floodlights used instead of track or recessed lights, are inexpensive ordinary items used extraordinarily. Colors are '60s coral, sea foam, and teal accents against white walls that take a backseat to nature's own constantly changing color scheme as seen through the glass brightly. 🌿

Top: Clerestory windows open interiors to treetop views.

Above: The curved roof emphasizes the contrasting verticality of the glass-lined front of the structure. A balcony-like deck adds tree-house ambience.

Part Two

COLORING THE NEW COUNTRY

CREATING ELEGANT SUN COUNTRY MOODS ALL THROUGH THE
HOUSE Elegant sun-country colors may be light and luminous,
bright but never garish, or neutral and nicely enhanced by rich texture. A
certain serenity, a prevailing calm and sense of sureness is color's contri-
bution to the new, dressed-up country look. There is nothing nouveau
about country's new richness, defined and underscored by color. Nor is
there anything especially vintage about the new mood, which is very much
today. There's a more-mature, savor-the-moment flavor to today's large
and small elegant country houses. Perhaps it's because the occupants
understand the need for and relish the opportunity to enjoy what is. This
is not to say that tradition is cast aside or that only fine, and therefore
expensive, things are welcome—far from it. Indeed, there's a much-more-
democratic acceptance of things from here, there, and everywhere. A
delightful move to eclecticism—of the sort practiced so deftly by Susan
Zises Green in which treasured objects from around the globe mix and
mingle with élan—is now more common. This high art of eclecticism
involves a sure sense of color and its unifying role. 𝄞 Color, of course,
is light and dependent on the nature and quality of light in specific
geographic areas. A particular color will not look or act the same in

Artist Alexandra Lotsch lets brilliantly colored fruit-shaped pendants on her dining room
chandelier and sconces make powerful eye-catching color statements. White paint trans-
forms all other surfaces in her dining room that hints of many countries.

Previous page: Designer Martine Colliander aims for an ethereal atmosphere with off-whites and light grays for background and light sun-country accents in her Solgarden Collection dining room for Lexington Furniture.

Above: Designer Lillian Bogossian splashes pretty Provençal prints with a dramatic dark background against bold yellow-gold walls in this bedroom that's chock-full of country comforts, such as the drop-leaf table put to new use.

different parts of the world. Light pastels, no matter how luminous, do not stand up to the intensely bright natural light in the South. There, stronger, more-passionate colors are at home. In New England, the all-white house is country crisp and rich. In the South, the all-white house is

For dramatic impact, designer Diana Bell looks to the stark contrast of black and white in a plethora of comforting country-style checks, toiles, and ticking-stripe patterns.

a stark, cold, and uncomfortable contrast to the vibrant surrounding color and light. In the North, the passionate pastels and earthy ochres so at home in southern Europe tend to look a little silly. Not even a neutral color will look equally at home in North and South. For that reason, it is very important to consider several color swatches—variations of the same

Mosaics designer Michael Golden creates a surround-country garden in straight-from-nature colors, replete with larger-than-life flowers in a tiny designer-showcase bathroom.

key color—when trying to decide just what color to use in a particular house or room. When choosing a paint color for her country-house living room on the front cover, artist Alex Lotsch did just that. "I took several swatches into that room and studied them in the changing light at different times of day for several cloudy and bright days, in daylight, and under lamplight," she says. When she finally decided on a particular robin's-egg blue for her living room, Alex did so with great confidence, knowing exactly how that color would look under any and all circumstances.

Light, bright, or neutral—what should your color direction be? The answer to that question involves a number of considerations. There's personal preference. Some might say that this is the first and last consideration. Others believe that a house speaks to the decorator, and that it is the decorator's responsibility to listen. Some consider space sacred and architecture supreme. Decoration should always enhance architecture. It should only try to change poor architecture and, then, only to correct some inadvertent flaw, to make the architecture as excellent as it was meant to be. Often, the greatest challenge is harmonizing personal preference and architectural demands! And it can be done, thanks to the infinite variety of colors instantly available, ready to whisk onto walls with the wave of a fairy godmother's magic wand. All one need do is interpret the walls' sometimes outspoken message.

This rich country-style bath in nice-and-easy neutrals gains a colorful view of a picturesque country landscape through a fantastic mosaic mural by designer Michael Golden.

Newly discovered ceiling paintings dictated the bright color scheme for Susan Zises Green's kitchen. Antique signs and collectibles add color.

When Susan Zises Green pulled down the plaster ceiling in her castle kitchen, she discovered incredible paintings of the surrounding mountains and barnyard creatures. Although she preferred white walls and had planned to have them in that kitchen, she took her cue from the paintings and introduced a rich bright teal.

To those who consider bright colors nerve jangling and luminous lights still too bright, neutrals are a nice solution. And because of the

Foolproof neutral backgrounds prove great foils for bright accents that can easily be changed in a matter of minutes to create new looks for new seasons.

incredibly wide and growing range of neutral tints and tones, these need never be boring. Neutrals prove over and over to be the strongest backgrounds for colored accessories that change with the season and always say elegant sun country.

Indeed, neutral-colored backgrounds provide a wonderful opportunity for texture, which allows for visual and intellectual relief and interest. And switching accessories in different textures can and ought to change from season to season. Nature, the great chameleon, is wonderfully accomplished at this. Springtime textures differ from those that draw our attention in the fall when plants mature and change. Why not follow nature's lead? An example in decorating might be something as easy as switching pillow covers. A willow-green-colored pillow, covered in pol-

ished chintz for the spring, takes on a fall look in a more heavily textured chenille or tapestry fabric.

What do the light, bright, and neutral colors that are right for elegant sun-country-style houses have in common? A clarity and purity that is never muddy, sallow, tired, wan, or wishy-washy. Elegant sun-country colors are rich, complex (secondary, never primary), fresh, vigorous, and young. They contribute to country's sense of renewal.

Opposite: Designer Nancy Fowler makes a strong color stand in a neutral room with yellow plaid swags for the windows and for the pads of interesting chairs. Fresh flowers and collectibles add interest.

Above: Warm-and-gentle patterns played out in the mosaic-tile backsplash by designer Michael Golden add dash to a country-in-the-city breakfast area. Carefully arranged plants and accessories spice up the monochromatic color scheme.

Think of elegant sun-country-light colors as vibrant impressionist colors that capture, then play back the sun. Sweden's "northern lights" whites do this. We see this in Solgarden (sun garden), the furniture collection by Swedish designer Martine Colliander for Lexington Furniture, whose design consultant is JoAnn Barwick, author of *Scandinavian Country*. Martine, in her own Stockholm shop, had redefined the eighteenth-century

96

Gustavian style by perfecting a warm white patina and making the style fresh and new. This new sunnier white brightens interiors, relieving the drabness of gray wintry days and satisfying an emotional need for sunshine—exactly what elegant sun-country "lights" should do! Of course, these lights are more than just a medley of whites. They're blues, pinks, yellows, greens, lilacs, corals, and more—always rich-bodied, clear, luminous, fresh, dignified, and fun.

Above: Contrasting dark-framed prints create a subtle focal point in a bright guestroom.
Opposite: All-white Solgarden (sun garden) furniture plays up a light gray-and-white scheme.

BRIGHTS

Elegant sun-country-bright colors are secondary and tertiary colors—never primary, never neon, never overly dramatic jewel tone. Think of complex hibiscus pinks and yellows and the glorious pink, blue, and pale green of full-blown hydrangeas—the broad spectrum of a garden full of zinnias, hollyhocks, snapdragons, and cosmos. Something quite wonderful about these colors connotes perpetual summer. They're especially magical when combined in printed textiles and wall coverings. Susan Zises Green uses these colors to perfection in her mountain-greenery home. Industrial designer Pilar Larraz uses these colors in a more graphic, stylized manner in her southern-comfort courtyard house in

French toile de Jouy bed skirt and draperies and an Italian cut-work tablecloth coexist happily in this sun-country bedroom.

Above: Designer Susan Zises Green uses morning-glory-pink bed hangings to create a delightful *lit-a-la français*.

southern Florida. Susan Jennings and Peter McMahon use these colors in an entirely different way in the tree house that they built. Truly, this palette offers infinite possibilities!

NEUTRALS

Neutrals take a strong stand in elegant sun country. Most often, they back off the decorating stage, giving nature full play. The Richardses' marsh-magic home and architect Michael Prodanov's seaside-serenity house are

Above: Lillian August furnishings in a medley of pale colors play up a sense of restfulness in a country living room. A sunburst mirror sparkles above the sofa.

excellent examples. Whenever nature is such a visible and powerful presence, a neutral palette makes great sense. It also makes good sense when one wants the utmost peace and quiet, perhaps relieved only by textured accessories or punctuated by colorful accents. Fortunately, there's a great range of neutral colors from which to choose. And there's the new trend of layering neutrals—that is, using not just one white, but many—or mixing many whites with grays and punctuating them with deeper colors that fill nooks and niches, as architect Vance Hosford does in his forest-glen house.

Opposite: A mosquito net above a wicker daybed creates an instant sleeping porch.

Above: Sun country goes global with furnishings from around the world.

Following Page: Lillian August mixes textures magically, contrasting lush fabrics.

Texture Terrific

Rooms without interesting textural contrasts are like land without water—desert dry and deadly dull. Textural contrast is a necessary ingredient, along with pattern and color, in any recipe for a successful room. Color, pattern, and texture are never used in equal amounts—the more of one, the less of the other two. How much texture is enough in a particular room? Remember that you're pitting rough against smooth, shiny against matte, small grains against large, and so on. Here are some examples:

* Pile raffia-covered or trimmed pillows on a natural linen sofa.

* Layer a sisal rug—with a nonskid pad—over a polished wooden floor.

* Hang art in heavily carved wooden frames against plain painted walls.

* In a neutral-colored room, add deeply carved or bright metal sculptures, framed mirrors, or framed art.

* Faux-paint gypsum-board walls by ragging, rolling, or strieing to imply textural depth.

* Add a collection of slick glass bottles, vases, candlesticks, or sculpture to a roughly surfaced tabletop.

* Introduce live plants—ivy, ficus, bromeliads, orchids, or cacti—in a variety of textures to any room.

* Create plant and dried-flower arrangements to suit— roses for a formal room, field flowers and tree branches for an informal space.

* Bring in found objects—smooth round pebbles from the riverbed, birds' nests, bits and pieces of rusted metal, driftwood, abandoned architectural remnants—they're all texture for the taking.

Part Three

GREAT COUNTRY ACCENTS

DECORATING WITH FAVORITE THINGS The more things change, the more we look to old favorites—with a twist! In the case of elegant sun country, the more elegant the room, the dressier the accessories. So, while many of the same things appropriate for any country-style room— chicken sculptures, quilts, baskets—are suitable themes for an elegant country room, the materials in which they are rendered are finer and fancier. Instead of parading in rustic pottery or pewter, roosters strut their stuff in porcelain, bronze, brass, or silver. Candlestick collections go from raw wood to bone china or colorful glass, like the ones in the Sterns' barn kitchen. Throw pillows in a country plaid are likely to be silk instead of cotton, damask instead of denim. ᧬ Confusion disappears in elegant sun country; calm-inducing order reigns. That means saying good-bye to clutter. Collections are fewer, and pieces are larger and more important. Less is once again more. ᧬ Painted accent furniture is more important than ever, but crudely executed work is out. Artistry and craftsmanship are today.

A Monet-like blue-and-yellow color scheme underscores the garden theme of this sunny dining room. Overhead, a stencil pattern enlivens the ceiling, adding interest.

Roosters and hens, favorite rustic-country-style icons, perk up elegant places, too.
It's difficult to trace the first time a rooster or hen image was used as a
decorative motif, but three exotic roosters decorate an eggshell porcelain
cup from China's Yongzbeng era (1723–35), now in the private collection of an Englishwoman. Walk past gift and accessories shops today, and
it's easy to spot these elegant creatures, sculpted life-size in pottery, porcelain, cement, and sterling silver; painted on wood and ceramic tile panels;
cut out of rusted tin; or painted in vibrant polychromes on metal. Country's favorite icon—that trumpeter of the dawn whose job sometimes is as
a weathervane adornment—can now be seen everywhere, even in elegant
sun-country interiors.

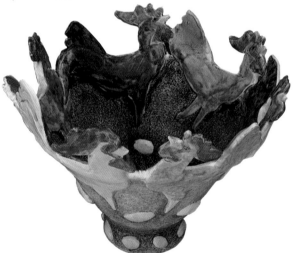

Fine porcelain ceramic roosters and hens appear to be hands-down
the favorite form for fancy interiors. And no single breed rules the roost.
Look for chic chick sculptures all decked out as white leghorns—fiery-
red combs with dramatically sweeping pure-white tail feathers; Plymouth
Rocks—somewhat like the leghorns but with less-dramatic tail feathers;
New Hampshire or Rhode Island reds; black-and-white speckled
Domineggers; or some purely fanciful breed known only to the artist.

Opposite: Roosters play ring-around-the-rosy in Marianna Roumell-Gasteyer's bowl.

Above: Roumell-Gasteyer's elegant rooster stretches his neck to crow about tea.

Sometimes, a rooster or hen sculpture is also an elegant teapot, especially in the hands of a creative artist such as Marianna Roumell-Gasteyer.

SUN FACES

The golden sun face is an ancient yet ever-new symbol of vitality. Since ancient times, motifs and patterns of the sun, the symbol of life, have decorated temples and shrines all over the world. A circle of dancing sun rays, sometimes surrounding a face, seems a universally understood and accepted symbol of power. France's Louis XIV called himself the Sun King and wore sun-king costumes in theatricals presented to his court. Court painters depicted him wearing a crown of sun rays. Louis was following in the path of Helios, the sun god of Greek mythology, also the wearer of a sun-ray crown.

The sun face in many guises continues to decorate our homes today. As clay plaques, sun faces hang on the walls of patios, terraces, and loggias; indoors, they hang in sunrooms and garden rooms and kitchens. As a

Ornately painted porcelain roosters dress up the hutch in a cheerful sitting area.

carved or painted wood or metal frame, it surrounds mirrors, paintings, or portraits and decorates living rooms, dining rooms, bedrooms, and baths. It is even possible to find an enormous sun-face clock to hang above an elegant country fireplace mantel.

Large-scale sun faces hang dramatically alone. Smaller ones can be grouped together or mixed with paintings in an eclectic collection. Wherever and however these ancient icons are displayed, they are elegant reminders of the importance of life itself.

Above: For added sparkle, designer Kim Barret hangs a glittering sunburst mirror above the headboard of a beautifully draped bed.

Opposite: A baroque sunburst above the mantel creates a dramatic focal point in a living room furnished by Grange with casual chic.

BLUE-AND-WHITE COLLECTIONS

Blue-and-white collections are the ultimate eclectic accessories that can be used at home or anywhere. Blue-and-white china is the decorator's dream accessory. Its arresting color, captivating shapes, and fascinating patterns go beautifully with all styles and periods. In fine translucent porcelain, blue-and-white is especially at home in elegant country houses. Not only is this ideal art a foolproof decorative accessory but, because of its history and endless variety, it is also an understandably addictive collectible.

The history of blue-and-white porcelain is a fascinating tale of the development of unique glazes and innumerable imaginative shapes and patterns. It stretches from the beginning of blue-and-white in China's Tang dynasty (618–907) until its popularity as a decorating staple today. In China's Song period (960–1279), pottery making became an industry employing full-time professional potters, allowing blue-and-white to be widely available domestically and throughout Southeast and Near East Asia. During the Yuan period (1260–1368), potters were skilled in using underglazes such as blues and copper reds. During this period, white-and-blue colors were totally amalgamated and suspended in the glaze, giving a unique softness to the color. In the Ming dynasty (1368–1644), the golden age of blue-and-white, the use of native cobalt, rich in manganese, was refined, reaching perfection in a deep, luminous sapphire blue.

The first blue-and-white with European decorative patterns was made for King Emanuel of Portugal in the early 1500s. In the sixteenth and seventeenth centuries, much blue-and-white was exported to Europe by the Dutch East Indies Company, which established an office in Canton. Blue-and-white became known in Europe as Cantonware. By the

Opposite: A collection of blue-and-white porcelain graces the wall and hutch in this enthusiastically furnished grand-country dining room by designer Jack Fhillips.

Following pages: Blue-and-white plates create a rich grouping above a Lillian August sofa.

Above: Lunéville has reissued this pattern that it originally created for Marie Antoinette.

1800s, several English factories were producing their own blue-and-white. Some Near East and European factories were producing copies of Chinese blue-and-white, but America continued to import from China. Today, fine blue-and-white is available from such French porcelain makers as Haviland in Limoges, and English companies that include Staffordshire and Spode. Inexpensive blue-and-white pottery known as Blue Willow was given away as premiums in the early 1900s in the United States, then blue-and-white popularity waned. But when a leading interior designer hung an arrangement of blue-and-white plates on the yellow walls of a 1970s interior, even Blue Willow became prized. To this day, timeless blue-and-white is all the rage!

FABULOUS FURNITURE

Easy-to-look-at pieces based on great old ones add elegant authenticity. Almost any furniture style goes in elegant sun country as long as it contributes to the dressed-up mood. It is even possible to mix in one peeling-paint piece

Above: Fantastic furniture often keeps secrets. This Irish Victorian side table from Baker, for example, has a mechanism that raises it to form a three-shelf Gothic étagère.

Above: An arresting cocktail table—like the West Indies colonial-style table by Milling Road—creates a natural gathering spot in a living room dedicated to quiet conversation.

Opposite: Woodland's Louis XV–style chair in a bold rooster print gives any room something to crow about.

as long as it doesn't switch the balance from dressy to dressed down. It's especially helpful to use one dynamic piece of furniture to transform a room from dull to dynamite. What makes a piece particularly interesting? Perhaps it's a side chair with an extra-tall or uniquely shaped back. It might be an exaggerated wing on an otherwise traditional wing chair. A dramatic polychrome finish, like that on Woodland's Italian pantry, can

add excitement. Painted motifs, such as those on French farmhouse furniture by Woodland or Habersham's garden-look furniture, can turn a piece into a focal point. Historic, authentic-reproduction furniture, especially the Borders Collection of unusual pieces from Scottish and Irish castles and manor houses—a part of Baker's Stately Homes Collection—is captivating. The point is, when you think country accents, think of adding an easy chair that's not only comfortable but attractive.

NATURE'S BOUNTY

Forget accessories that feature beautiful fruits and vegetables—use the real thing!
It's only natural to plop flowers fresh from the garden into a vase and on a
table or to pluck a bunch of fruit and pile it on a plate or in a basket for
the kitchen counter. These simple gestures can look elegant indeed. It's
also elegant to follow the example of baroque-era paintings and pile
extravagant mounds of glorious fruits, vegetables, and flowers on huge
trays. Palm Beach interior designer Jack Fhillips does this with real
aplomb and artful effect. The trick is to:

* ❋ Use the freshest fruit, flowers, and vegetables—and only
  for a brief period.

* ❋ Choose containers that are just as rich-looking as the
  fruit—like an over-scaled porcelain platter, lacquered
  tray, painted-wicker or French wire basket, silver box,
  or glass bowl.

Opposite and above: Designer Jack Fhillips uses nature's bounty—fantastic fruits and plants—as very tasteful, highly decorative, and ultimately edible accessories. His secret: heaps of various fruits for contrast.

* Think texture. Mix shiny with matte surfaces. Tuck in tree branches, twigs, or leaves with fruit. Add polished stones, shiny seashells, or colored marbles. Tie a silk ribbon around a bowl, vase, or basket handle.

* Adopt a more-is-better attitude. Never stop at two of anything when four will look better.

* Layer your arrangements. Circle your container of fruit or vegetables with smaller arrangements, such as ceramic cups filled with baby's breath or Queen Anne's lace. Add large chunky candles to the mix.

* Get more attention by using exotic fruits or vegetables or unusual combinations.

* For a dressy living room, use a decorative vegetable in a fancy container.

* Leave fruit and vegetables in edible condition. Do not fold, bend, spindle, or mutilate them so that they go from display to dump. Plan to have your cake and eat it, too, so to speak. Practicality can be very elegant.

WINDOW DRESSINGS

Add to the interior view with window finery. Architecturally rich windows need not be dressed when privacy or light control are not issues. But just the right window treatment adds an extra dimension to even the most artful architecture. It may add exciting pattern, intriguing texture, or a softening line that turns the window into a focal point or finishing touch.

It is not necessary to invent a new and different window treatment. Traditional window treatments have proven themselves over time. New fabrics and trims update these timeless treatments, keeping them fresh and beautiful.

No window treatment should look contrived. Simplicity is the key to true elegance. The simplest of draperies, together with unique or special hardware, will transform a plain-Jane window into a focal point. For example, plain beige linen panels with tab tops hung over an iron pole

Designer Honora Hillier cleverly includes books as decorative accessories and makes a charming window seat an inviting reading nook. After sundown, swing-arm lamps light up the printed page.

Above: Designer Lillian Bogassian adds panache to old-fashioned window shades by covering them in a Provincial print and treating hems to pointedly pretty diamond shapes.

sporting decorative finials will add more than enough drama to a quiet guest room in a country house. Simple curtains shirred over painted wooden poles are unfailingly delightful. Add wide ribbon tiebacks for country charm, and add basic blinds for light control. Some blinds, such as matchstick, also lend texture.

Above: Designer Elfriede Williams plays up the Midsummer Night's Dream theme of a sunporch cum dining room with streams of sheer curtains held in place by gilt stars.

Elegance need not be stuffy. Combine witty hardware and a simple swag for elegant, yet memorable, whimsy. That's exactly what happened when a clever designer used three bathroom faucets to create window hardware for a smart silk swag above a plain double-hung window in an old-fashioned country-house bathroom. 🌿

Part Four

Elegance Al Fresco

Dressing Up Outdoor Living Spaces Outdoor living is a vital part of celebrating summer, the season that sun-country-style decorating extends to all year. Increasingly, that sense of season is being extended year-round for homeowners everywhere. Some homeowners, such as Richard Stern (Barn Beautiful), do not hesitate to don a parka and dash out to the patio to put steaks on the barbecue—even when the ground is covered in snow! The key to decorating an outdoor world is to think of outdoor spaces as an aesthetic extension of one's home. Elegance relies on a sense of harmony. To achieve harmony between house and grounds, furniture should be chosen in a style compatible with the architecture of the house. If the house is rustic, one should choose rustic furniture. If it's modern, homeowners should select modern furniture. If a house is more traditional than either rustic or modern and the homeowners find themselves with wooden furniture that's a bit too rustic, they should paint it! That's exactly what the Sterns did. Old pine picnic furniture wasn't quite right for the new, sophisticated, soft-green exterior chosen to unify the existing cottage and barn addition. Using leftover house paint, the Sterns

---

Palm Beach designer Jack Fhillips dresses up the great outdoors by piling on pillows, adding a lightweight throw (even tropical country can get chilly), and lighting a candle.

transformed ugly and no-longer-appropriate furniture into furniture that blends in! This is a quick, easy, and inexpensive solution.

The house's scale should be considered when selecting furniture. If it is a large manor house, large-scale furniture that looks as though it belongs should be chosen. If the house is a cottage, furniture in a smaller but not necessarily delicate scale will seem more suitable.

Grange-woven tropical-lounge furniture graces a loggia that is protected from the elements yet open to views of surrounding gardens. Natural sunshine is aided and abetted by colorfully painted walls and containers filled with brightly blooming plants.

Color choice is important for outdoor furniture. It should complement the exterior walls of the house. It should also coexist harmoniously with nearby plantings and especially with flowering plants and trees. This goes for accessories, too.

Furniture arrangement is just as important outdoors as indoors. There's nothing convivial about a row of chairs strung along a porch, patio, or pool. Chairs can be grouped around a coffee table just as in a den. Side tables can then be set up for drinks and books, preferably where shade is available. Seating in a hideaway nook or niche is best for those who seek privacy or welcome respite. A loggia or gazebo can provide shel-

Beautiful all-weather furniture, such as Brown Jordan's Provence tables and chairs that look dressy but require no fuss, makes it easy to entertain al fresco. The graceful trellis pattern in the chair backs makes the dining area the focal point of the pretty patio.

ter from the weather and the sun. A long bench or lonesome hammock are just the places for a quiet snooze. Comfort, convenience, and elegance are a happy trio outdoors as well as inside and make family and friends feel welcome and well cared for.

QUICK-AND-EASY DECORATING IDEAS
FOR OUTDOOR ENTERTAINING

Entertaining family and friends al fresco can be done easily and elegantly without spending a fortune. Here are some quick-and-easy dress-up ideas:

✻ Provide ample casual seating for conversation as well as dining. Handsome foldout chairs with sled bases are welcome—chairs with feet can sink into the lawn.

✻ If everyday lighting is inadequate for an evening gathering, consider the following: hang old-fashioned kerosene lanterns out of children's reach and away from plants; use chunky candles shielded from the breeze with hurricane globes; place torch stakes in the ground, protected so that no one stumbles into them;

Above: Rattan garden furniture by Grange looks casually at ease on the lawn of a handsomely colored home. Accessories are just as light and portable as the furniture.

Opposite: Dramatically shaped arches create mystery and romance in an open room where a round table and deeply cushioned chairs make for pleasant dining and game playing.

and string tiny white electric lights—like those used for holidays—everywhere!

✳ Use large potted shrubs or trees to create boundaries that enhance the sense of room and coziness on open terraces or patios.

✳ Hang decorative plaques—in weather-wise ceramic tile, metal, and painted wood—or other items on an otherwise blank and boring wall. Richard and Stephanie Stern hung a row of painted-metal soldiers on the wall of the screened porch in their barn.

✳ Cover old lawn-furniture cushions with wash-and-wear pillowcases for a quick switch from faded to fabulous.

✹ Plan your color scheme just as you would for an indoor affair. If flowers are blooming nearby, take your color cue from them. Use tablecloths, napkins, china, and candles in the same colors as the blossoms and cut some of those blossoms for your centerpiece.

✹ Trim a tattered table umbrella with a string of silk flowers.

✹ Add a sisal or flat-weave (dhurrie or kilim) area rug to a seating area or beneath the dining or picnic table. These are lightweight and easy to roll up and return indoors.

✹ Arrange outdoor furniture just as though it were indoors; that is, create cozy conversation areas and leave plenty of passage space around the dining table.

✹ Create a buffet or drinks table by covering a picnic table in a king-size, wash-and-wear sheet or a dhurrie or kilim rug. Back it up to a wall or wall-like screen of trees. Place a colorful floral arrangement at the back side of the table and arrange drinks or food as you would if you were entertaining indoors.

A boldly painted, long, narrow table set with colorful dinnerware fits neatly on this porch for open-air dining.

Resources

Here are a few favorite furnishings sources for a country-style house and garden. Most sources are available almost everywhere. Their furnishings are affordable and elegant.

BOOKS

McMillan, Patricia Hart, and Katharine Kaye McMillan. *Home Decorating for Dummies.* Foster City, California: IDG, 1998.

McMillan, Patricia Hart, and Katherine Kaye McMillan. *House Comfortable.* New York: Perigee, The Berkley Group, 1996.

McMillan, Patricia Hart, and Katherine Kaye McMillan. *Sun Country Style.* Salt Lake City: Gibbs Smith, Publisher, 1999.

Manroe, Candice Ord. *Window Treatment Styles.* Lincolnwood, Illinois: Publications International, Ltd.

Muraro, Michelangelo, and Paolo Marton. *Venetian Villas.* Cologne, Germany: Konemann, Bonner Str.

Phillips, Betty Lou. *Provençal Interiors: French Country Style in America.* Salt Lake City: Gibbs Smith, Publisher, 1998.

Ross, Pat. *Formal Country.* New York: Viking Penguin, 1999.

Designer Kim Barrett brightens a bedroom with a sky-blue scheme that has touches of gold and a basket of fresh-from-the-garden flowers.

Wagoner, Ed. *Furniture Facts.* Tulsa, Oklahoma: J. Franklin Publishers, Inc. (c/o Selling Retail International, P.O. Box 14057, Tulsa, OK 74159; [1-800] 444-6141), 1997.

Witynski, Karen, and Joe P. Carr. *Mexican Country Style.* Salt Lake City: Gibbs Smith, Publisher, 1997.

Witynski, Karen, and Joe P. Carr. *The New Hacienda.* Salt Lake City: Gibbs Smith, Publisher, 1999.

Zoglin, Ron, and Deborah Shouse. *Antiquing for Dummies.* Foster City, California: IDG, 1999.

MAGAZINES

These favorite magazines—on newsstands everywhere—are treasure troves of information and feasts for the eyes.

British Country Homes & Interiors
011-44-171-261-6895 ph
011-44-171-261-6405 fax

Country Home
(1-800) 374-9431

Country Living
(1-800) 888-0128

House Beautiful
(212) 903-5000

Maisons Cote Sud
Newsstands

Southern Accents
(1-800) 882-0183

CATALOGS

American Quilts
(1-877) 531-1619
Handcrafted American quilts in a wide array of patterns and colors.

A circle of mosquito netting adds instant romance to American Standard's whirlpool-in-the-round. Books for a read-and-lounge session decorate the back wall. Overhead, a demilune window admits sunlight.

Designer John Michael Telleria added pizzazz to country comfort by covering fancy French chairs in a ticking stripe and pulling them up to a glass-topped table.

Gardeners Eden
(1-800) 822-9600
Fresh, charming designs for indoor and outdoor use.

Garnet Hill
(1-800) 622-6216
Uniquely designed bedding and other household items.

Golden Valley Lighting
(1-800) 735-3377
Custom lighting fixtures in designs that are special.

Gump's Interiors by Mail
(1-800) 248-8677
Captivating designs—many from Asia—to add a special touch to rooms throughout the house.

Horchow Home
(1-800) 395-5397
Items designed with classic good taste for use throughout the house.

IKEA
(1-800) 225-IKEA
Clean-cut, common-sense furnishings made in Scandinavia for use throughout the house.

Janovic Plaza
(1-800) 772-4381
Great sources for paints, wallpapers, fabrics, and window treatments.

Smith & Hawken
(1-800) 776-3336
Ideal source for outdoor furnishings that have great style and personality.

Smith + Noble Windoware
(1-800) 248-8888
A storehouse of blinds and shades in a wide range of textures, colors, and styles.

Ballard Designs
(1-800) 367-2810
Unique, classically designed items for use throughout the house.

Chambers Linens
(1-800) 334-9790
Fine, affordably priced linens in interesting patterns and colors.

Ceramic artist Marianna Roumell-Gasteyer's racy radishes dance merrily across a platter.

Spiegel
(1-800) Spiegel
A big catalog and convenient source of well-styled, well-priced furnishings.

Studio Steel Custom Chandeliers
(1-800) 868-7305
Smartly styled, custom lighting fixtures.

Sundance
(1-800) 270-6617
Western style that mixes well with sun country.

This End Up Furniture Co.
(1-800) 627-5161
A great source for affordably priced, good-looking, simply designed furnishings.

DESIGN CENTERS

Visit the many country-style showrooms in these design centers with your designer or architect, or use one of the center's on-call designers. Call for an appointment before you go.

Design Center of The Americas (DCOTA)
Dania, Florida
(954) 920-7997

Designers & Decorators (D&D) Building, New York Design Center
979 - 3rd Ave,
New York City, New York
(1-800) 732-3272

Pacific Design Center
(1-800) 732-7261
Web site: www.pacific.com

MANUFACTURERS

These manufacturers make great products and provide useful information. Call for literature and the name and location of their nearest retail representatives. Check their advertisements in your favorite decorating and remodeling magazines and click onto their Web sites.

American Standard's country sink-in-a-sideboard is a witty and dressy focal point.

DeTonge
Valbonne, France
33-93-95-80-00
A wonderful source for authentic,
antique-style, painted, country
French furniture.

Grange
(1-800) Grange-1
(212) 685-9057
Leading maker of classic French
styles updated for today's lifestyles.

Harden Furniture
8550 Mill Pond Way
McConnellsville, NY 13401-1844
Web site: www.harden.com
Well-made furniture without
gimmicks, just right for today's
country living.

Lexington Furniture
(1-800) LEX-INFO
Web site: www.lexington.com
Lexington invented the weekend-
furniture look and continues to
create trendsetting country-style
furniture.

Martex
(1-800) 458-3000
Web site: www.martex.com
Super bedding for casual but smart
living.

Schreuder Paint
from Fine Paints of Europe
(1-800) 332-1556
Extraordinary paint colors available only from this maker. To see is
to believe!

Souleiado
Tarascon, France
33-90-91-01-08 fax
Maker of legendary fabric that's
synonymous with southern France's
sunny decorating style.

Elegant country mixes an English chair, French chest, and tropical table.

Wellborn Paint & Color
(1-800) 228-0883
(1-800) 432-4067 (New Mexico)
Rich velvety-looking paint in special colors that astound.

RETAIL STORES

ABC Carpet & Home
New York City
(1-800) 458-2414
Everyone's favorite home-furnish-
ings destination in New York City.
The flea-market aura and vintage
café make shopping an adventure.

Pier 1 Imports
(1-800) 447-4371
Web site: www.pier1.com
A fun place for impulse shopping and
spontaneous decorating. Furnishings
are bright, colorful, dynamic, and
sensibly priced.

Pottery Barn
(1-800) 922-9934
Chic simple furnishings make this
the place for good-looking kitchen,
dining room, and accessory basics.

Roche Bobois
183 Madison Avenue
New York City, NY 10016
(1-800) 972-8375
French-made furniture in a variety
of styles and periods.

Toujours Provence
(DeTonge and Souleiado)
85 SE 6th Avenue
Delray Beach, FL 33483
(561) 330-0561
(561) 330-0562 fax
This charming little shop is just the
place to find painted French
furnishings without traveling to
Provence. Stay for lunch or snacks at
the bistro.

PHOTOGRAPHIC CREDITS

Colophon
The body text and subheads are set in Bernhard Modern. Chapter openings are set in Boulevard and captions are set in Trade Gothic.

Previous page: Designer Jack Fhillips loads a cabinet with colorful majolica and walls and windows with pattern in this country-style breakfast room.

Above: This light-filled and eye-catching corner of a Philippines home is furnished with Raphael Legacy Designs Sun Country Collection.

Opposite: A Fhillips-designed dressy bedroom looks country, but not cottage.

Overleaf: Phillips adds country ambience with gingham checks and floral pillows.